A Trilogy on Race and Power:

- The Village of Nigger-Nigga

- CORRUPTION... A Precondition for Power

- Nigger Music

by Harold L. Price

Table of Contents

Introduction

In the following work, there are three separate but related works. The first work focuses on the power of language, the specific example being that of the so-called "*n*" word. There are several key thoughts and questions worth keeping in mind as you read the first work, *The Village of Nigger-Nigga.*

First, the more "*forbidden*" or "*taboo*" something is, the more powerful it becomes. In view of that, the question arises: "Who benefits from the negative power created by preserving the "*n*" word as a "*taboo*"?" Primarily, if not exclusively, so-called "*white*" or "*non-black*" people. In other words, those who would use it as a "*weapon*" to hurt others emotionally. And who suffers from the negative power created by preserving the "*n*" word as a "*taboo*"?" Primarily, if not exclusively, so-called "*black*" or "*non-white*" people.

Conversely, who would benefit by neutralizing the negative meaning/use of the word "*nigger*" *and*/or giving it a new and positive meaning? Virtually, all of society in general, both here in America as well as the world at large.

Although the first work, *The Village of Nigger-Nigga*, is a work of fiction in the strictest sense, there is a significant degree of linguistic truth in principle regarding the message of this short story. For example, unlikely as it may seem in terms of the feasibility of converting the "*n*" word from something negative to a positive, linguistically speaking, language is more than sufficiently capable of accommodating such a change.

The second work, *Corruption...a Precondition for Power*, addresses the matter of power in general. In terms of the message in this essay, it can readily be applied to the first work, *The Village of Nigger-Nigga*. For example, one can get a fairly clear idea from this essay as to what type of person would want to preserve the negative meaning and use of the word "*nigger*".

Finally, the same application of the essay on power can also be readily applied to the second essay, *Nigger Music*.

The Village of Nigger-Nigga

The village of Nigger-Nigga was in the same boat as America at large...at least until recently. This village also had a different name...until recently. However, recently something strange happened in this village. And that strange event changed this little village in ways that have since made it very different from the rest of America. And as a result, the people of this village have since been joyously living in the true spirit of those iconic words *"Free at last, thank God Almighty, free at last!"* It is also because of this strange event that the people of this village were inspired to change the name of their village to Nigger-Nigga.

This village's name change was kind of like in the ancient times and tradition of the Biblical Old Testament in which a person who changed for the better - or "turned over a new leaf", so to speak – commemorated that wonderful change by also changing his or her name. Paul is a classic example of such a change. He originally went by the name of Saul. It was also during that time in his life that he was a devout Jew and devoted persecutor of Christians. But then he had a life-changing spiritual encounter and experience with Jesus. That caused him to "turn over a new leaf". In his case, that meant he not only stopped persecuting Christians. He also became a Christian himself and changed his name from Saul to Paul to commemorate his momentous change. Moreover, he became so devoted to his new life as a Christian that he eventually was made a saint and has since been known as *Saint Paul*.

Well now, the people in the village of Nigger-Nigga had an equally life-changing experience. Here's what happened as it was told to me by the village elders of Nigger-Nigga. I'll tell it from the time before, during and after this village's life-changing event.

As noted earlier, in the beginning, this village was the same as the rest of America. You had various groups like "red, yellow, black and white". And yes, like the rest of America, the people in this village also had their racial divide and all of the unpleasantness and duplicity generated by such a divide. For example, in the old spirit of the duplicity of "political correctness", no one ever uttered the "n" word in public or directly to any black person. However, in private, the unbridled use of the "n" word was as ubiquitous as the air itself. This was true of white people, other non-black people and even black people themselves.

Then one day, there appeared a man, a very strange and enchanting man. He was strange because he openly used the "n" word…but he used it to address everyone, "red, yellow, black and white". However, such strange behavior was at the same time irresistibly enchanting. No one, "red, yellow, black or white" quite knew how to respond to such behavior. And because everyone was also constrained by the rules of "political correctness" as those rules were understood by these villagers, no one dared to challenge, chastise or question this odd fellow in his

2

open and ubiquitous use of the "n" word. However, in private, everyone – old and young, "red, yellow, black and white", male and female, rich and poor, educated and uneducated – confronted this odd fellow about his open and ubiquitous use of the "n" word. And since the village population was so small, within several months, every villager capable of speaking and understanding this violation – albeit odd and enchanting - of the rules of "political correctness", had managed to steal a private and discreet opportunity to confront this odd fellow one-on-one.

By the time I was told everything by the village elders, everyone had already shared his or her private conversation with this odd fellow. According to the village elders' account, all of the villagers reported very similar conversations. So, I was reminded that, although I was being given a generalized or composite account of the all conversations, it was an accurate representation of the conversation each villager claimed to have had with this odd fellow.

"Hey Joe," the villager said to the odd fellow, once they were alone. "So, what's with this "nigger…nigga" business you keep sayin' to everybody?"

"I'll be more than happy to explain it," said Joe, "…on one condition…or maybe a few conditions…"

"What condition or conditions?" the villager asked.

"Well, one condition for sure is that you first explain to me, define for me exactly what a 'nigger' is.

"Are you serious?"

"Yes. Are you trying to avoid the question?"

"No…but, I mean, everybody knows what a 'nigger' is…which brings up the question of why you call everybody 'nigger'."

"As I said, first tell me what a 'nigger' is. You say that everybody knows what a 'nigger' is. But, well, what if I don't

3

know? What if I'm from a foreign country or another planet? How would you explain or define a 'nigger', so I would be able to identify them and limit my use of the word to them?"

The villager began to chuckle. It seemed a somewhat nervous chuckle. "You're serious...?"

"Completely serious."

"Okay, here it goes. A 'nigger' is a black person," the villager said with an air of impatient authority in his voice.

"And what is a 'black' person?"

"What?" the villager responded in disbelief.

"What is a 'black' person?" Joe repeated.

The villager let out with a heavy sigh of frustration while maintaining an expression of disbelief on his face. "A *'black'* person!" the villager repeated emphatically. "You know...what they used to call 'Negroes'... 'colored' people."

"You mean there are people who are not 'colored'?" Joe responded.

"Of course!" the villager replied.

"So, there are people without any 'color'? Do you mean, like, 'albinos'?" Joe asked.

"No, no, no!" the villager uttered impatiently. "I mean like 'white' people...people like you and me."

"But I'm not 'white'", Joe responded. "If I had to describe myself, I'd have to say I'm something more along the line of 'beige' maybe. But even that's not really accurate, because... well, when you say 'black', 'colored'...are you referring to 'skin' color?"

"Yeah...I guess," the villager replied.

"Now I'm confused," Joe said.

"Why?"

4

"Because I've studied biology and according to biology, all human skin is described as a kind of 'pale white'. In other words, 'colorless'...no color at all in human skin."

"What?!" the villager uttered. "Well then, how do you explain...just look at your skin and mine...And now look at Big Bill over there across the street. He's as black as the Ace of Spades. Now, are you tellin' me you don't see that difference...between him and us?"

"Of course, I see the difference. But it's not a 'skin' difference," Joe insisted.

"Then what the hell kind of difference do you think it is, Joe?"

"He just has more melanin than you and me," Joe explained.

"More what?"

"Melanin. It's a dark brown chemical under the skin. And it's the melanin's color that reflects through the skin. The more melanin you have, the darker it makes your skin look."

"Okay then," the villager said. "So, 'black' people must mean people who have more of that melanin stuff than me and you."

"Are you sayin' that Tony D'Angelo is 'black'? Joe asked.

"Of course not! Tony's Italian," the villager replied. "I mean, he's a red-blooded all American...Italian-American, if you want to be technical about it."

"Well then, since he looks darker than Frankie Adams, does that mean Frankie is not 'black' either?"

"No. Frankie's 'black'. In fact, his family's ancestors were slaves..."

"How come he's 'black' but Tony isn't? Is it because Frankie is the descendant of slaves?"

"I don't know", the villager confessed. "I guess so."

5

"So, it isn't so much a matter of 'skin color' but ancestry. Is that what you're sayin'?"

"Not real sure at this point...maybe a combination of things...like the way you look plus whether your ancestors were slaves," the villager said.

"You mean American slaves as in people from Africa who were brought to America as slaves?"

"Yeah, maybe that's it. I'm pretty sure they're the only ones who get called 'nigger'."

"But what about the ones with less than $1/32^{nd}$ of African blood?"

"What are you talkin' about now?" the villager responded.

"They say, or at least they used to say, that if a person had less than $1/32^{nd}$ of African blood, then, that person qualified as 'white'," Joe explained.

"Never heard that, but I guess if that's true, then okay."

"So, if everybody knew that a person had less than $1/32^{nd}$ of African blood, that person would be accepted as 'white'?" Joe asked.

"Well...I kinda doubt that...I mean, maybe if nobody knew, maybe. But if everybody knew, I think people would still consider him a 'nigger', no matter how little African blood the person had."

"At that rate," Joe said, "everybody must be a 'nigger'."

"What?!...Why do you say that?" the villager responded.

"Because," Joe added, "according to science, all humans originally came from Africa. And therefore, all humans have African mitochondria in their blood."

"Mito'...what?"

"'Mitochondria'. They are a part of the cells that make up our body. We all have this African mitochondria in our blood. So, if you're human, you're African too..."

6

"Be that as it may," the villager remarked, "a 'nigger' is not just someone with this African stuff in their blood. They also are the descendants of slaves."

"Does that mean the 'black' people in Africa aren't niggers...since neither they nor their ancestors were slaves?" Joe asked.

"I'm not sure...now you're confusin' me," the villager said.

"And what about the so-called 'white' Americans?" Joe continued.

"What about us?" the villager asked.

"A lot of 'us' are the descendants of slaves too," Joe replied.

"What?!" the villager uttered.

"Oh yeah!" Joe said. "Many of 'us' from Europe had ancestors who were 'slaves' back in the day...in Europe."

"When was that?" the villager asked.

"During the so-called *Middle Ages*...from around 476 A.D. to 1453 A.D. "Our" ancestors were called "*serfs*"...but that was just a clever way of saying slave...to get around the Church policy forbidding "*slavery*".

"So...you're sayin' that for nearly a thousand years...white people in Europe had other white people as slaves?" the villager asked in astonishment.

"You got it! By the way, 'blacks' were slaves in America from 1619 to 1865. In other words, 'blacks' were slaves for 246 years compared to 'whites' in Europe, who were slaves for closer to 1,000 years."

"Hmm...," the villager uttered while rubbing his chin.

"Plus...," Joe continued.

"Gees...you mean there's more?"

"A bit. Not all 'blacks' were slaves. In fact, some 'blacks' were slaveowners."

"I never heard anything about that."

7

"Not surprising," Joe remarked. "Our history books seem to treat such facts as State secrets. Anyway…it seems all of us are 'niggers'. Or, if not, at least some 'black' people – such as the ones whose ancestors were never slaves, including the 'blacks' whose families have always been in Africa – can't be considered 'niggers'…unless you considered the whole human race as African…'black'…and, therefore, all humans are 'niggers'."

"Joe," the villager interrupted in a tone of irritation, "so what's the point you're trying to make here?"

"Why not call all of us 'niggers'?"

"What good would that do?" the villager asked.

"Well, for one, it would make us more honest. But more so, it could end the unpleasantness that comes with the way the word 'nigger' has been used traditionally."

"I'm not quite following what you mean," the villager said.

"If we admit and accept that we are all human, all of African descent, all 'niggers'…then the word 'nigger' would end up with a new meaning."

"That being?"

"Human being. Then, we could add 'brother' and 'sister'," Joe added with a smile.

"'Brother' and 'sister'?"

"Yes, the way it is used by the Quakers and your so-called 'black' people. The way they use 'brother' and 'sister' simply means 'fellow human being'. It's just another way of saying we're all related to each other like brothers and sisters related by blood…which, it turns out, we really are."

"But 'nigger' also means 'stupid', 'ignorant' and 'uncivilized'? So, 'niggers' are not only the descendants of American slaves, they are also 'stupid', 'ignorant' and 'uncivilized'," the villager persisted.

8

"Well…some so-called 'black' American descendants of Amercian slavery may also be all that…'stupid', 'ignorant' and 'uncivilized'. But not all of them. At the same time, there are also a lot of so-called 'white' American descendants of European slavery who are 'stupid', 'ignorant' and 'uncivilized' too, as in your so-called 'white trash' or 'trailor trash'…and they all have African blood running through their veins as well. And if the whole truth be told, all people are, and always have been, 'stupid', 'ignorant' and 'uncivilized' to some extent…including you and me."

"So, you're sayin' no matter what the meaning of 'nigger' is, it applies to all Americans?"

"It would certainly be impossible to prove otherwise…especially considering all of the cross-breeding that's gone on in America since the first African slaves in 1619 in Jamestown, Virginia," Joe added.

"What do you mean by that?" the villager asked.

"Before the American Civil War, many Southern and a lot of Northern so-called 'white' Americans had sex with so-called 'black' slave women. And there were many, many babies that resulted from all of that so-called 'inter-racial' sex. During and since that time, so-called 'whites' have also interbred with other so-called 'whites'. But some of those so-called 'whites' were actually the descendants of 'inter-racial' sex passing as 'white'."

"How many?" the villager wondered out loud.

"God only knows. What is more certain is that even the so-called 'white' immigrants since the Civil War have interbred with 'white' Americans who were here before and during the Civil War. And again, Lord knows how many of them already had 'black' blood, were in fact 'blacks' passing for 'white'," Joe continued.

9

"So, you're sayin' any 'white' person could actually be 'black'?"

"Yes…knowingly or unknowingly…To be sure, any way you define 'nigger', it would apply to nearly all – if not all - Americans. And that being the case, why not use the positive meaning of 'nigger' meaning simply 'brother' or 'sister'?"

"That doesn't seem very realistic. I mean, too many people, black and white, are used to the original meaning of the word," the villager remarked.

"Doesn't matter. If enough well-meaning people, black and white, openly called each other 'nigger' meaning brother or sister, and each new generation was taught what we have been discussing, I think eventually, the positive meaning would become standard," Joe responded. "Plus, think about the negative effects of the alternative."

"What alternative are you talking about?" the villager asked.

"The 'taboo' approach…based on the principal of 'political correctness'," Joe replied.

"Oh," the villager uttered. "You mean the 'taboo' against using the 'n' word in public?"

"For example, yes."

"But how is that a negative thing?"

"Well…think about it for a minute…for one thing, some 'taboos' often make the 'forbidden fruit' more tempting, more irresistible. And a violation of the 'taboo' can also cause the victim of the violation to feel even more upset. Think about how children react to ridicule like being called a name."

"You mean like in my preschool class, when little Tommy calls his black classmates 'Blackie'?"

"That might be a good example, depending on how little Tommy's 'black' classmates react to being called 'Blackie'", Joe replied.

10

"Usually ends up with them fighting," the villager said. "The black students are really sensitive to being called racial names like that."

"Um hmm," Joe grunted. "What if you explained to your class why your 'black' students are 'black'?"

"I'm not sure that would make any difference…I assume you're talking about that melanin chemical you mentioned earlier?" the villager remarked.

"Yes, but be sure to include one of the main jobs and effects of melanin."

"Which would be…?"

"One of its main jobs is to absorb one of the sun's poisonous rays, known as ultraviolet light. When the ultra violet light touches the melanin, the melanin does two things. One, it absorbs and neutralizes the ultra violet light. Two, the melanin cells double. One effect of that is that it increases the black color of the melanin reflecting through the skin."

"Did you just explain how people get a suntan?"

"Yes. And that is one way to turn the 'taboo' of being called 'Blackie' into something positive."

"I'm not following what you mean?'

"Who spends tons of money on suntan lotion and hours of discomfort exposing themselves to the sun in order to get a suntan?"

"Ah ha!" the villager uttered. "White people!"

"And they do all that to end up looking like who?"

The villager chuckled. "Black people…I'll be damned!"
"So, it's actually a positive thing to be black."

"And therefore, to be called 'Blackie'", Joe added. "So, I wouldn't make the futile attempt to forbid the use of the nickname 'Blackie'…Instead, I would encourage using it openly.

11

But every time it is used, I would also require the user to explain why the name represents an enviable benefit."

"Actually, benefits. After all, black people get to save money by not having to buy suntan lotion. They don't have to suffer hours of discomfort lying in the sun..."

"And therefore, 'black' people have less chance of suffering from sun burn, which is the result of being exposed to too much sun," Joe further noted.

"By the way, Joe, what about that more recent version of 'nigger' that a lot of 'black' people use with each other?" the villager asked.

"You mean 'nigga'? Joe asked.

"Yeah...what about that?'

"Well, as I understand it, 'nigga' just means something like 'dear friend'. So, anyone, 'black' or 'white' could use that to refer to anyone who is a dear or close friend."

As indicated earlier, it was actually only over the course of many discussions and village meetings that all of the preceding ideas were covered. However, in the end, the majority of villagers agreed to adopt and use the positive meaning of 'nigger' and 'nigga'. In addition, to re-enforce this new tradition, a village majority soon after also voted to change the village's name to *Nigger-Nigga*. So there you have it as was told to me by the village elders of *Nigger-Nigga*. And on any given day, as you walk the streets of *Nigger-Nigga*, you will hear its village residents joyously addressing each other as *nigger*, *nigga* or both, depending on circumstances. For example, earlier today, I heard a man named *Dick* and a woman named *Kitty* greet each other as they passed each other on Main Street:

"Good morning, *Nigger Dick*", Kitty said with a joyous smile.

"And a Good morning to you too, *Nigger Kitty*", Dick responded with a joyous grin.

This then is why this village is so different from the rest of America, why its residents go about their daily lives with their mind, body and soul clearly expressing the joyous words: "*Free at last, thank God Almighty, free at last!*"

CORRUPTION...
A Precondition for Power

"Power tends to corrupt, and absolute power corrupts absolutely." That is what Lord Acton claimed in 1887. However, that claim is profoundly incorrect. Power does not corrupt. Rather, power requires that the power seeker already be corrupt. In other words, being corrupt is a pre-condition for the pursuit of power.

Nonetheless, simply being corrupt is not enough to acquire, keep or increase power. In addition to being corrupt, at least two other conditions are required. One is competence. That is, a person has to be good at being corrupt. Otherwise, the would-be power seeker will achieve no more than membership in the club of the "dumb and dumber". Besides competence, another condition may also be necessary, at least some of the time. That condition is pure and simple "luck", being in the right place at the right time.

Again however, the supreme or absolutely basic requirement is that the power seeker must already be corrupt. If not, then competence and luck are worthless. For example, consider the matter in terms of Snidely Whiplash and Dudley DoRight. Imagine both running for President of the United States. Snidely is already corrupt and willing to do anything necessary to win. In contrast, Dudley is limited in what his moral values would permit him to do. Consequently, Snidely would be free to bribe, blackmail, lie, cheat, steal and murder to the extent allowed by luck and his competence to succeed in carrying out any such actions. Dudley, on the other hand, would have to play by the rules. Not being corrupt, Dudley simply would not be able to stomach doing any of the things that Snidely would be willing and able to do. It would be like having two teams of basketball players, each with the talent of a Michael Jordan. However, one team would be "competently" corrupt and the other virtuous. The team of corrupt players would do such things as bribe and blackmail the referees and scorekeepers, even murder or threaten to murder them if they did not do whatever the corrupt team demanded. At the same time, the virtuous team would simply not be willing or able to do anything except play by the rules. At such a rate, it would not take a rocket scientist to predict that the winner in any such scenario would be Snidely and the corrupt team respectively.

Given the above noted pre-condition of corruption, it is obvious that and why Lord Acton's statement about power is incorrect and profoundly so. To be sure, the pre-condition of corruption is a far more viable idea than Lord Acton's view, in terms of making sense of why truly good, decent people remain consistently powerless (or end up dead, if unbeatable despite playing by the rules), while corrupt people end up exclusively and consistently with all the power. Socrates expressed a similar, if not the same, idea. He said that the Unjust (people) make themselves look just while making the Just look unjust. Still another similar, if not the same, idea was also expressed by a linguist taking literary license with a Biblical passage.

He said: "'The rain falls on the Just and the Unjust'…but mostly on the Just, because the Unjust steal the umbrellas from the Just."

Incidentally, a few important, obvious points should be noted. One, no one is perfect. Therefore, the "good, bad and the ugly" are qualities that can be observed in all human beings. However, the 'bad' tends to dominate in the character of some people, while the 'good' tends to dominate in others. So, when referring to "corrupt" people, it should not be assumed that such people are necessarily lacking any "good" qualities. Likewise, it should not be assumed that those we think of as "good" or "decent" people, are without any "bad" qualities. It's more like "corrupt" people usually behave corruptly, if necessary, in order to get what they want. Whereas "good" or "decent" people usually choose to behave in a "decent" manner by, for example, "biting the dust" or giving up the chance to get what they want, if it requires that they hurt someone in order to get what they want. The "key" point here is "usually". (For example, students who "usually" get an "F" on their tests, fail and are thought of as "failing" students, even if they get an "occasional" "A" on a test. Conversely, students who "usually" get an "A" on their tests, pass and are thought of as "successful" students, even if they get an "occasional" "F" on a test. The "failing" student is not a "perfect" failure and the "successful" student is not a "perfect" success. However, realistically or in practical terms, especially when dealing with people when such qualities as honesty are needed and desired, we all, given the option, will avoid doing business with people known to be "usually" "dishonest" while seeking instead to do business with people known to be "usually" "honest".) So, when reference is made to "corrupt" and "good" people, the reference should not be taken to mean that there are "absolutely" "corrupt" people or "absolutely" "good" people. (Every dog has its day…and everyone occasionally has a bad hair day.) We are not talking here about any "God-versus-the Devil" level of "Good and Evil", just the naked ape in varying degrees of nakedness.

In any case, corruption can and does take advantage of opportunities in virtually every area of human social life. However, there are three areas in particular that tend to be favorite stomping grounds for corruption. They are conflicts (such as wars), poverty and "race" (as in "black" and "white" people). As will be asserted, all three of these conditions are contrived realities created for the sole purpose of feeding the appetite for power, whose pre-condition is "corruption".

Let's begin with "poverty". Poverty is real, but not inherent. In other words, although seemingly inevitable, it is not necessary. Rather, it is a contrived reality and essentially for one reason…power. However, to get that power - in such forms as "profits" and lucrative salaries – requires widespread, continuous corruption. Some of the main players in this "con" game are such entities as business people, politicians and bureaucrats.

Poverty is "big" business. The profits are huge. Take for example the "Welfare" system. Every welfare system "requires" a building or complex of buildings. This becomes a great source of profits for the construction industry. However, that industry includes far more than just construction companies. Those companies do not make their own steel and concrete. Rather, such materials are made by still other companies. Once the building is built, other companies are paid to furnish the building with furniture such as tables, desks, chairs and lamps, while still other companies are paid to provide such items as computers, filing cabinets, paper, pens and pencils. Then of course, there are

17

the companies needed to provide such commodities as electricity and heating fuel. All such businesses make huge profits by servicing the welfare system. All of them have a vested interest in the continued existence of poverty. All of them also maintain an army of lobbyists such as lawyers and PAC's (Political Action Committees) at local, state and federal levels. These latter groups, also, obviously have a vested interest in the continued existence of poverty.

In addition to the business aspect of poverty, there is also the "bureaucratic" aspect. The top bureaucrats of such poverty agencies as the welfare system, make huge salaries. Moreover, such bureaucracies include an army of lower ranking employees, who receive salaries as well as "benefits" such as health care and pensions. These benefits also "benefit" big business such as insurance companies (health care plans) and financial institutions (pension investments).

Finally, there are the "fat cats", aka "politicians". Besides receiving their own salaries and benefits (health care, pensions, etc.), politicians get to feed as well like vampires on the enormous amounts of taxes taken from all those taxed salaries and profits generated by the vast "poverty" system. Of course, in order to justify and preserve this "poverty" system, it is necessary to maintain a large and constant population of poverty-stricken people. Hence, the large army of recipients enrolled in the welfare and other "assistance" programs within this vast "poverty" system. Incidentally, big business and politicians benefit further from the money and other welfare benefits given to this huge army of poverty-stricken people. For example, these welfare people also must pay rent and shop. This spending adds to the profits of business as well as to the taxes from those profits and the salaries of those who work for landlords and store owners. Much more could be included in the matter of how

18

profitable poverty is. However, suffice it to say that all those benefitting from poverty, obviously, have a vested interest in the preservation of poverty and, therefore, of a large class of poor people.

Although perhaps less obvious, it is most significant to focus more on those at the top of this food chain in order to understand more clearly how poverty is a contrived reality created to feed the appetite for power. This point will be addressed in greater detail after first addressing the other two areas of interest also identified earlier as contrived realities created to feed the appetite for power. Those two remaining areas are "conflicts" and "race". I will continue next with "war" as an example of "conflicts" and conclude with "race". Then I will focus in greater detail on these three areas (poverty, conflicts, race) as three of the most common contrived realities created to feed the appetite for power.

"War". The lyrics of a popular song once expressed: "War! What is it good for? Absolutely nothing!" Unfortunately, that is far from the truth. Indeed, the truth is that war is perhaps the greatest means for generating the kinds of profits and benefits identified in connection with poverty. In fact, war generates not only much greater profits but many more benefits as well, at least, from the viewpoint of those in need of satisfying their appetite for power.

To begin, consider this aspect of war. At least in modern times, it is absolutely true that there are two distinct groups always involved in war - those who declare and profit from war but never actually fight in the war...and those who actually fight in the war but never declare it or profit from it. For example, President Wilson declared war to enter America against Germany in World War 1. However, Wilson himself did not fight in that war. In fact, he never even served in the military at all. Twenty-four years later, President Roosevelt declared war to enter

19

America against Japan, Germany and Italy in World War 2. Yet, like Wilson, Roosevelt also neither fought in that war and never served in the military. The same can be said of America's corporate leaders who "serviced" the two world wars. For example, Henry Ford and Pierre S. Dupont made obscene amounts of profits as industrial suppliers for the American government during World War I. Yet, neither one of them actually fought in World War I. In contrast, millions of other (common) Americans fought, died, were wounded, etc. in both wars. Yet, none of them either declared or made profits from either war.

Another insidious "benefit" of war, has to do with population and economic development. War "kills two birds with one stone". On the one hand, war reduces population by claiming the lives of so many of the millions who actually fight in the wars. On the other hand, war also stimulates economic development due to the need for increased industrial production. So, as the population of the living decreases, so does the population of the unemployed. "Happy days are here again!"

Finally, there is the contrived reality of "race". The simple truth is that "human" races do not even exist in the scientific or biological sense. This has been an accepted fact among scientists for decades, if not centuries or even millennia. The basic motive for the "con" job of "race", is that it provides a very effective strategy for the power brokers to "control" their subordinate populations. That strategy is "divide and conquer". For example, in America, as long as poor and middle class "whites" and "blacks" are kept at each other's throats, they are also kept from uniting against the power brokers screwing both of them. Incidentally, the power brokers are completely aware that "human" races do not exist, especially not the ridiculously bogus version of "race" that the common masses are (mis)led to believe in.

At any rate, at this point it is worth commenting on the three examples of poverty, "war" and "race" in terms of how they relate to corruption and power. First, all three of these areas of human social life are completely avoidable. For example, poverty is not an inherent principle of reality, especially not for a "self-proclaimed" Christian nation like America. Whether as a Christian resisting such sins as avarice while obeying the first commandment and the Golden Rule, or simply as a good, decent human being or Dudley DoRight, there would be no moral justification for one person to hoard a million dollar income while another human being is living in poverty. Of course, the immediate knee-jerk reaction of the millionaire is to utter the diversionary boogeyman accusation that such a suggestion to share is the godless idea of communism or socialism. If that is true, then, Christianity must be a form of communism or socialism. And American kindergartens too, since "sharing" is a basic value taught in kindergarten (e.g., "Everything I needed to know, I learned in kindergarten.") Not only does hoarding millions for oneself have no moral defense, it is also not a practical necessity. Simply put, no one needs a million dollar income to survive or even to maintain a materialistically comfortable lifestyle. On the other hand, if a person is addicted to power and corrupted in character, that corruption will enable such a person to behave in any way necessary to satisfy the insatiable appetite for power.

A less flattering but perhaps more revealing term for a corrupt character might be "psychopath" or "sociopath" as in the likes of Charles Mansion. Few would have any problem accepting such a term in reference to Charles Mansion himself. However, there seems to be precious little difference between the

21

corrupt character of Charles Mansion and that of the pimps who orchestrated the Enron scam. Their behavior was no less sociopathic in their selfish attempt to acquire obscene amounts of money for themselves and knowingly at the cost of destroying the lives of untold numbers of everyday families. And what about the many other power brokers such as Nixon, McCarthy (politicians); J.Edgar Hoover, Oliver C. Wenger (bureaucrats); Ford, Dupont (business people or "captains" of industry); and the many other politicians, bureaucrats and captains of industry throughout history, American history in particular?

As with poverty, so it is with conflicts such as "war". Every war ever fought, could have been avoided. The "causes" of every war, were problems (whether real or contrived) that could have been solved by peaceful means. That is, war is no more inherent or necessary as a solution than is poverty as an economic condition. However, war is, like poverty, obscenely profitable. For example, the DuPonts made a quarter billion dollars in profits from gunpowder sales to the American/Allied governments during World War I. A quarter billion dollars by today's standards would be more like a quarter trillion dollars in profits.

The pernicious lie of "race" is the third noted commonly used form of corruption as a means to power. Perhaps one of the most revealing commentaries on this form of corruption is the book *Killers of the Dream* by Lillian Smith. Her work is a compelling insight in and of itself but even more powerful when coupled with the scientific position on race such as was expressed by the world's leading scientists through the United Nations Educational, Scientific and Cultural Organization (UNESCO) in the 1950's. Regarding this 1950's UNESCO position, the idea of "human" races is so completely rejected that the collective recommendation of the participating scientists was to eliminate the use of the term "race" altogether when referring to the human

22

groups (e.g., red, yellow, black and white) normally identified as "human races". Obviously, that recommendation continues to fall on deaf ears. At any rate, the benefits derived from this insidious lie also include obscene amounts of profits and other forms of opportunity to acquire, gain and increase power (economic, political and social). Finally, in the following essay, "race" will continue to be one of the primary areas of focus while addressing the broader issue of corruption and power in greater detail.

Nigger Music

The following commentary focuses on a modern example of the American or Anglo-Saxon strategy for power. That is, the ancient Germanic belief that "Might makes right" or the deification of worldly "power". Bear in mind that devotion to this belief in worldly power, includes any and all conceivable forms of power such as fame, glory and wealth. Furthermore, this strategy for worldly power uses "truth" the way a pimp uses a prostitute. For example, if it helps to gain, keep or increase one's power, then, the truth is used in the name of God. Or, if necessary, the truth is combined with lies. ("Deception" was one of the most well-known skills of Odin, the ruling Germanic god.) Other times, outright lies may be told. In that case, the strategy of repetition is used. As Göbbels (Goebbels), Hitler's heinous Minister of German Nazi propaganda, is purported to have said: "If you repeat a lie often enough, people will begin to accept and believe it as the truth." In fact, the bigger the lie, the greater is its chance of becoming accepted as the truth, especially if it is constantly repeated by official authorities as the truth. This strategy is straight out of the most infamous textbook on power, *The Prince*, by Machiavelli. However, it is worth remembering what Machiavelli himself said was the source of his advice on how to gain, keep and increase one's power. That source was history itself! The recorded history of what rulers have always actually done to gain, keep or increase their power. That history includes such strategies as: "lie, cheat, steal, murder, pretend that you don't, and deny that you do". In the following commentary, the focus is on power in the form of glory, fame and wealth. The strategy is a combination of truth, a mixture of truth and lies and outright lies repeated so often that many people have come to accept these lies as truth.

More specifically, then, I will shed some light on a number of issues that have so far been reprehensibly shed in a false light. This will include some of the many documented facts that support and validate much, if not all, of the following commentary. Even more assuredly is this commentary's validity supported by the force of reason (i.e., rational/logical thought). At any rate, I will leave it to others who desire more, to provide a more comprehensive presentation of the relevant supporting facts and/or force of reason validating the present commentary. My primary mission is to help get certain ideas into the public consciousness before the bullshit "revisionist" historical record about the issues at hand becomes "holy writ".

First, the matter of Rock'n Roll. This music was originally called 'nigger' music. This was before the creation of the "Great American Fraud" known as "Elvis". I recall a video documentary on white southern reaction to this music during the 1950's. There was a group of white protestors demonstrating in front of a white-owned restaurant. They were protesting the white owner including "nigger" music in the selection of songs his customers could pay to hear on his jukebox. One protest sign expressed the view that "if you don't want to serve niggers in your restaurant, then, don't allow nigger music in your restaurant!" In another documentary film, a white minister also addressed the issue of "nigger" music to his congregation. He preached that the niggers were using this nigger music to drag white people down to the level of the nigger. He added that this nigger music was "evil" and that this "*evil*" was "in the '*beat* '". He meant, that the "*evil*" was in the "*rhythm*" of the music, which had previously been referred to first as "*nigger*" *music*, then as "*Rhythm*" *and Blues* and finally as "*Rock and Roll*". Moreover, this "*rhythm*" or "*beat*" was "*evil*", because it aroused "*sexual*" feelings. More on that later in this commentary.

In any case, this was during the 1950's and this "nigger" music was sending white people into a panic. Why? Predominantly for the following reasons:

1. White kids were going crazy over this "nigger" music.

2. This music could not be stopped and the white kids couldn't be stopped from listening to it.

3. This unstoppable music threatened to turn "niggers" into a popular, famous and wealthy group of people.

4. Because of the above three reasons, this "nigger" music also threatened to turn white kids – most especially white 'girls' – into "nigger-lovers".

As one source put it, "The changing musical styles listened to by American teenagers was first evident in Memphis. Most of the jukeboxes…in Memphis hangouts during the early 50's [before the "creation" of Elvis] were stocked with songs by black artists." This same source also quotes Sam Phillips - the white producer of Sun Records and "creator"/promoter of Elvis – as saying: "…distributors, jukebox operators, and retailers knew that white teenagers were picking up on the feel of the black music." This same source further notes that, despite the money being made from this black [i.e., "nigger"] music, there was also a certain concern among white people. That concern was - according to what Phillips is further quoted to have said – "We're afraid our children might fall in love with black people." (For example, at one concert, a white teenage girl kissed Chuck Berry [for which he was arrested]; while in a documentary film interview, a southern white teenage boy said: "All I wanted was to be black on a Saturday night.") This out-of-control popularity of Rock and Roll ("nigger" music) among white teenagers was before "Elvis" was even created by Sam Phillips. Such documented records completely contradict the defenders of "Elvis" who make the slick claim that "Elvis" was responsible for popularizing Rock and Roll (among white teenagers). Again, the music was already popular among whites (at least white teenagers).

The need for and role of an "Elvis" had more to do with the concern of white parents that their children – especially, their daughters – were "…fall[ing] in love with black people (especially, black males); and with the white male lust for power through the usurpation of the fame and fortune that would otherwise go to blacks (especially, black males). Accordingly, to kill two birds with one stone "…[Sam] Phillips decided that he needed a white performer…Phillips found…Elvis Presley." Still another source in a video documentary recorded Phillips making

27

a remark to the effect that he could make a million dollars (on this "nigger" music), if only he could find a white boy to imitate it. This same documentary then notes that within a year after making this remark, Phillips "discovered" (i.e., "created") Elvis…"The Great American Fraud".

To be sure, this so-called "nigger" music had been created years before Elvis was even known to exist. (For example, one of his first and biggest hits was his 1956 imitation of Hound Dog, which had already been originally done as a "hit song" by the famous "Rhythm and Blues" singer, Big Momma Thornton…in 1953.) Again, certainly by 1951 (three years before Sam Phillips "discovered" Elvis), this "nigger" music or "Rhythm and Blues", had already become popular among white and black teenagers.

Again, others called it "R&B" or "Rhythm and Blues". Finally, in 1951, a white (Jewish) DJ named Alan Freed decided to call this music "Rock and Roll." His reason for choosing the term "Rock and Roll", is never explained in the standard bullshit slick "white" revisionist" histories of "Rock and Roll." However, that reason has not yet been completely buried by the white revisionist historians. For example, one source puts it this way: "…Alan Freed…disc jockey …[coined] the term rock and roll in 1951…[in order] to avoid the stigma attached to R&B [Rhythm and Blues] and so called race [nigger] music…[In so doing]…Freed opened the door to white acceptance of black music, eschewing [rejecting] white cover [imitation] versions in favor of the R&B originals." A few examples of the "white cover or imitation" versions, were Pat Boone's pathetic imitation of "Blueberry Hill" by Fats Domino; as well as Elvis Presley's clownish imitation of Tuti Fruti by Little Richard and, as already mentioned, "Hound Dog" by Big Momma Thornton.

At this point, it is worth contrasting the historical record just noted, with the propaganda of a white revisionist record on the history of rock and roll. In an article on Sam Phillips ("creator"/promoter of "Elvis"), there is a presentation of some background information leading up to the point where Sam Phillips (also the white producer of Sun Records in Memphis, Tennessee) first had "Elvis" in his Sun Records recording studio for an audition. This same source makes it clear that it was at this point in history when Phillips realized he may have found his "Great White Hope" to imitate and market the "nigger" music. According to this same source, that moment occurred on "Monday evening, July 5, 1954..." The article then adds that as a result of this epiphany of Phillips, "Rock 'n Roll was born!" Again, this was 1954, three years after the white (Jewish) DJ, Alan Freed, had first used "...the term rock 'n roll in 1951..." as a more tactful term for R & B (Rhythm and Blues) – i.e., "nigger" music. Furthermore, Elvis' first hit song, Heart Break Hotel, didn't happen until 1956 – which was five years after Alan Freed had coined the term "Rock and Roll". That was, also, a year after Chuck Berry's hit song, Maybellene and Little Richard's hit song, Tutti Frutti (which Elvis would later "cover" ["imitate" – or attempt to imitate]). In addition, regarding Chuck Berry's hit song, Maybellene, Rolling Stone magazine stated the following: ""Maybellene" is considered one of the pioneering rock and roll singles..."

In view of such documented facts, how could Elvis have given birth to Rock and Roll when it had already been born ten years before Elvis had even been "created"; had been renamed (from Rhythm and Blues to Rock and Roll [by Alan Freed in 1951]) three years before Elvis ; and had itself already given birth to ""Maybellene"... one of the pioneering rock and roll singles..." a year before Elvis' first hit song?

Still more disgusting is such nauseatingly perverse propaganda as one particularly unfathomable, air-head remark of the Beatles' John Lennon, who claimed regarding Rock and Roll: "Before Elvis, there was nothing." Even Elvis himself acknowledged that "...rock n roll was here a long time before I came along'. 'Nobody can sing that kind of music like colored people'. 'Let's face it: I can't sing like Fats Domino can. I know that'." And in another public statement, "...when a journalist referred to him as 'The King', Elvis gestured toward Fats Domino, who was taking in the scene. 'No', Elvis said, 'that's the real king of rock and roll'."

To be sure, it was their clownish imitation of Chuck Berry's hit song, Roll Over Beethoven - not any Elvis song - that would be the Beatles' first hit. If Lennon was so awed by Elvis as the "god'/"king" of Rock and Roll, why did he try imitating Chuck Berry instead of his "god'/"king" Elvis. Seems Lennon was as mindlessly and transparently hypocritical as he was blasphemous.

In any case, Freed rejected the white versions of this music, such as Pat Boone's imitation versions of Fats Domino's songs – and "Elvis'" imitation versions of Little Richards' songs. For his efforts, Alan Freed would soon spend the rest of his life suffering from the white revenge of the U.S. Department of Justice, which left Freed broke, endlessly in and out of court, and out of work, all of which eventually led to his death while still in his 40's. (Incidentally, Freed's crime was "payola" and "income tax evasion". "Payola" was the illegal but common practice of paying disc jockeys to play, and thereby promote, certain records. Alan Freed was never investigated for "payola" until after he had

30

begun refusing to play the "white" imitation versions of the "nigger" music. In any case, since these "payola" payments were not reported income [due to their being illegal], no income tax was ever paid on the "payola" income. So, Freed was "busted" for "payola" and "income tax evasion" – but only after it was clear that he was not going to give in to the pressure to play the "white" imitation versions of the "nigger" music.)

This persecution of Alan Freed sent a clear message: "It is forbidden to use the original and authentic "nigger" versions of the "nigger" music now commonly referred to as "Rock 'n Roll". Instead, only the "white" bread imitation versions were to be played on the radio and sold in stores". This "stacked card" arrangement guaranteed that all the white "cover" or "imitation" versions would be heard and sold far more than the original, authentic "nigger" versions they imitated. And it was only on this "rigged" basis of "more" sales, that "Elvis the Imitator" was fraudulently crowned with the contemptible title of "King" of Rock 'n Roll.

It is also worth noting at this point why it is so pathetic and clownish even to suggest that a white person created rock and roll. First, consider the term itself: "rock" and "roll". This was a black American slang expression that meant "to copulate". In other words, "to have sex", "to screw", "to fuck". The term dates back to the 1920's even before the time of such "R & B" black singers as Big Momma Thornton (whose 1953 hit "Hound dog" would later be "covered" or "imitated" by "Elvis" in 1956). Alan Freed (the white [Jewish] DJ who replaced the term "R & B" with the term "Rock 'n Roll") was aware of and picked up this black American slang expression (rock and roll), because he hung around black people in the 1940's and 1950's.

Alan Freed chose this term (rock and roll) for good reason. It strongly hinted at the nature of this black music's rhythm and the pattern(s) of the dances created to go along with that music. To put it explicitly, both the music and the dances were sexual in nature. "Rock" meant to rock your hips back and forth like a rocking chair. "Roll" meant to roll your hips like when swirling a hoola hoop. These two motions (rocking and rolling the hips) combined to mimic the body/hip motion used during/for sexual intercourse. Again, both the music and dances were - and still are - symbolic of the spirit of sexual intercourse.

Such music and dances were, in other words, echoes and shades of ancient African fertility rites. Studies in anthropology (e.g., Durkheim) have long since documented the claim that "religious" song and dance are the last pieces or vestiges to be lost or exorcised from the memory of a people cut off from their native culture. Numbers of first generation slaves attempted to pass on the essentials of their native culture. Yet, ultimately, within a generation or two, native languages and other more advanced specific cultural behavior were lost. However, the more dynamic spiritual disposition and basic forms of expression were effectively passed on through song and dance.

The obvious similarity between African fertility song and dance and African-American song and dance is especially clear when the two traditions are contrasted with each other. This was actually made possible at least once through a performance by an African-American dance troupe in the mid 1970's at the Pennsylvania State University main campus. During its performance, this African-American dance troupe divided itself into two groups. The first group was clad in traditional African forms of dress as they performed traditional African dance patterns to the rhythm of traditional African percussion instruments (e.g., bongos, etc.). The second group was clad in various forms of dress popular among African-Americans from the 1920's up to the 1970's. To accomplish this task, the second group was further divided into smaller groups. The first of them was clad in the "rags" (e.g., "zoot suits") popular among black Americans in the 1920's. They performed the dances created by black Americans during the 1920's to the music created by black Americans during the 1920's. Next came a group representing the black American dress, song and dances of the 1940's (e.g., "swing"). Then came the 1950's (Bee-bop/R & B), the 1960's ("soul" music) and finally the 1970's ("disco").

The grand finale was the performance of the African and African-American styles being blended together. The dancers paired up with each other. The African partner performed the African dance patterns while his or her African-American partner performed the African-American dance patterns of the time period of his or her "rags".

The music alternated back and forth from the traditional African percussion rhythms to the music of the different eras of African-American music. The rhythms and dance patterns of the African and African-American groups were virtually indistinguishable.

It is crucial now to review what was dominating the white American scene in America from the 1920's throughout the 1950's (the 1950's being the period when the term "Rock 'n Roll" - and "Elvis" - became popularized). The dominant influence among white Americans during this period of time was, in a word, "Victorianism".

It is when this fact (the dominance of "Victorianism") is contrasted with the essence of "Rock 'n Roll", that the white "revisionist" history of "Rock 'n Roll" becomes so obviously and clownishly contrived. First, the contrast exposes a basic dialectical opposition in sexual orientation. Blacks were branded with the scandalous reputation of being "sexual" animals (e.g., "once you go black, you can never go back"; Birth of a Nation;

etc.). Whites identified themselves with the standard of "sexual purity" (e.g., "no sex before marriage"; "sex only for making babies - not for pleasure, especially not for women"; etc.). In other words, blacks were sexually unrestrained while whites were neurotically wrapped and restrained in sexual straight-jackets.

It was this white neurotic, if not sociopathic or even psychotic, preoccupation with sex that gave rise to research on sex such as was conducted by Kinsey as well as Masters & Johnson…research which focused primarily on "white" Americans. It was also this same sexual dysfunction that eventually led to the so-called "sexual revolution" of the 1960's. That revolution was by and for "white" Americans (and black Americans were their role model).

Second, there are other telltale signs conveniently omitted in the white revisionist histories of rock and roll. For example, there was the age-old common expression that "blacks had rhythm, whites had no rhythm". This, incidentally, was a view expressed most commonly by white Americans themselves, at least until they began to lust after the profits and prestige from rock and roll. Then, they began to fabricate such frauds as "Elvis", "blue-eyed" soul brothers (e.g., the Righteous Brothers), "rubber" soul (e.g., the Beatles), "Rock" (vs. rock and roll), "Hard" Rock, (vs. rock and roll), etc. Still later, whites were also miraculously transformed into being the creators and models of the black dance form previously denigrated with such labels as "dirty" dancing. After the decision for a "hostile" take-over" of rock and roll, the idea of "dirty" dancing was repeatedly associated with the clownish, spastic, pathetic imitation of "dirty" dancing by "Elvis" on the Ed Sullivan Show. (Repeat a lie often enough, and people will accept it as the truth.)

In any case, the "dance" aspect of rock and roll is itself another telltale sign exposing the contemptible revisionist histories of rock and roll. For when blacks created the music of rock and roll, they also created dance patterns to go with the music. Perhaps the most famous example of this song-and-dance combination was The Twist. No popular dance (the Twist, Pony, Jerk, Monkey, Slop, Shimmey, etc.) performed by the masses to rock and roll music, was ever created by whites. Perhaps it is the difficulty in trying to claim a white as the creator of these rock and roll dances, that explains why the white revisionists of rock and roll history focus on the "music" while conveniently omitting the inseparability of the song and "dance" patterns inherent in rock and roll.

(Incidentally, both the song and dance known as The Twist, were created by a black man, Hank Ballard. However, his original version was considered too "raw" and he too "dark-skinned" to use him and his version of The Twist. Unfortunately however, for the likes of "Elvis", Pat Boone, etc., The Twist occurred when the Civil Rights movement, JFK, etc. were sweeping the nation. Nonetheless, the times were still not ready for the blackest of blacks. The influence of Alan Freed pushing for the original black versions of rock and roll, along with the growing influence of the Civil Rights movement, made it no longer "politically correct" to continue using "white" imitators such as "Elvis" and Pat Boone to "cover" the original black versions and performers. However, it was still an era dominated by a "color" caste. That is, "if you're white, you're all right; if you're brown, stick around; if you're black, get back". Consequently, the "brown" skinned Chubby Checker ["if you're 'brown', stick around"] was chosen by white record producers and promoters to "cover" the song and dance known as The Twist. Even Chubby Checker's version caused a national "scandal". The original by the dark-skinned Hank Ballard ["if you're black, get back"] was considered simply far too sexually "raw" – especially since Ballard was so imposingly dark-skinned [Chubby Checker was what was called a "high yellow" black].)

At any rate, while white revisionists have persistently – and to a great extent, successfully – attempted to create a fraudulent history of rock and roll, it is interesting that they, as already noted, have almost completely avoided attempting to do so with the dances that blacks created to go with the rock and roll music they created. However, even in the dance arena, some attempts have been made to revise the dance aspect as well, if only by innuendo…at least so far. In other words, no claim was ever attempted explicitly to credit "Elvis" or any other white with the rock and roll "dances" created by blacks. Nevertheless, the white revisionists do seem to have made at least one attempt to "suggest" that the sexual character of the rock and roll "dance" form was created by "Elvis". This attempt - still ongoing - has been in the repeated reference to "Elvis'" "scandalous" gyrating of the hips and how he was "censored" on TV (the Ed Sullivan Show) from the "hips" down. At the same time, blacks (e.g., Motown) were strategically being forced to come up with more "toned-down" (e.g., Supremes, Temptations, etc.) dance steps that were more "civilized".

Nonetheless, if one looks at the film recording of Elvis' "scandalous" dancing, it looks clownish. In his vain and pathetic attempt to imitate black (rock and roll/"dirty") dancing, he looks like he suffers from some sort of nervous disorder that causes him to thrash about in an uncontrolled frenzy of uncoordinated spasms. A slicker and more recent attempt to "revise" the history of black song and dance, came with the movie Dirty Dancing. Although Patrick Swayze displayed notably greater coordination than Elvis, he was still "acting". That is, there were no spontaneously improvised dance moves. It was all so tightly choreographed that it seemed stiff, artificial. Yet, the idea and image of a white male "dirty" dancing, reinforced the fraudulent notion of "Elvis" as the creator of such dancing.

However, even in the movie Dirty Dancing, the truth could not be fully buried. For example, perhaps the one song most associated with that movie and the image of "dirty" dancing, was the black (rock and roll) song Do You Love Me? by the Contours (circa 1963). At the time of that song's initial popularity, American Bandstand was still on the air. In fact, I clearly recall the Contours appearing on American Bandstand to sing their song and dance to it at the height of that song's popularity. In contrast, the white teenagers' lack of "dirty" dancing on American Bandstand at that time, was clearly displayed and recorded. Their notable "lack" of "rhythm" (to include "dirty" dancing) was still being acknowledged in that era as typical of how white people "danced" (i.e., "no rhythm"). Yet, twenty years later, a white male (actor Patrick Swayze) is portrayed in the movie Dirty Dancing as a "white" male master of "dirty" dancing during the early 1960's time period of that movie. In reality, during that time period, only blacks were performing their black ("dirty") form of dancing (and being disdainfully looked down upon as "animals" by whites a la *Birth of a Nation*, *Reefer Madness*, etc.)

Whites never contributed one significant iota of original creative input to the music or dance forms of rock and roll. To be sure, Elvis was certainly no less than a patent fraud. His "King" (of rock and roll) status was as rigged as the election of Bush as president in the Fall of 2000. That is, his "King" status was based on the number of records he sold. However, the "revisionist" histories of rock and roll conveniently avoid noting that Elvis sold so many records simply because blacks were deliberately and systematically denied the same degree of recording and distribution opportunities. Indeed, Elvis himself said "...rock 'n' roll was here a long time before I came along. Nobody can sing that kind of music like colored people." If the playing field had been level, it is unimaginable that Elvis would ever even have been noticed. He certainly would not have been so commercially successful as to achieve the statistics of the "mega" sales that serve as the basis for the propaganda of the white revisionist histories of rock and roll in which he has been relentlessly and shamelessly crowned as the "King" of rock and roll…even as its "Creator" as well as a "Master" - if not "Creator" - of "dirty" dancing. As for his popularity (the "craze" of females screaming and fainting, etc.) at the sight of "Elvis", it would not be unreasonable to bear a few potentially relevant facts in mind. One, Elvis failed his audition on the Arthur Godfrey Show (1956). Two, the Dorsey Brothers introduced both Frank Sinatra and Elvis. Three, Frank Sinatra's promoters "paid" white female teenagers to "scream, faint, etc." at the sight of Sinatra. Such staged realities might also be kept in mind for Elvis as well as "Beatlemania".

At any rate, Elvis was a patent fraud. And he knew it. He had no compelling talent for the black music known as rock and roll. In fact, many have insisted that his style of music be called "Rockabilly" ("Hillbilly" music with a hint of rhythm borrowed from rock and roll.). He was certainly neither "King" nor "Creator" of either rock and roll music or the black dance forms that went with the music. Indeed, Elvis, like other whites of the time, was socially, culturally and psychologically enslaved in a state of "Victorianism" - which put them at the other end of the spectrum of the "raw" sexuality and sensuality of rock and roll song and dance. Whites were as likely a creator of rock and roll as blacks were of the Germanic language known as English.

Perhaps most objectionable and repugnant about all this, is that rock and roll was born out of the history of black suffering and our creative response to that suffering as well as rising above

38

and overcoming that suffering. Gospel music and the blues were respectively religious and secular therapeutic forms of expression of our grief. Rock and Roll (or "Rhythm and Blues") was also a secular and therapeutic extension of the blues but in a much more joyous and playful form of expression. For a white to be credited with the creation of what blacks created out of the "blood, sweat and tears" of suffering at the shamelessly brutal hands of whites, is something one could only expect from "spiritual thugs", "spiritual thieves and con artists" Odin…Elmer Gantry… acquisition through Inquisition…you get the picture?

No? Well, just in case, here is a brief summary of the salient historical facts:

1. Rock and Roll (aka "nigger" music) is one of the musical forms or styles created by Black or Afro-Americans within the musical tradition of Black or Afro-Americans.

2. Rock and Roll (aka "nigger" music) existed and was popular among black and white American teenagers years before the appearance of "Elvis" Presley. (Even Presley himself stated this fact.)

3. "Elvis (Presley) was created for the 2-fold purpose of:
   1) Diverting white American teenagers - especially white American teenage girls - away from glorifying black Americans - especially black American males; and
   2) enabling white American males to usurp or appropriate for themselves the fortune and fame that otherwise would have been acquired by black Americans - especially black American males.

4. The title of "King" (of Rock and Roll [aka "nigger" music]) was bestowed upon "Elvis" based on the record sales and media promotion of "Elvis" resulting directly

39

from the rigged (corrupt manipulation of) restrictions aggressively imposed on the record sales and media promotion of the black American creators and master performers of Rock and Roll song and dance (aka "nigger" music and "dirty" dancing).

5. In transparent attempts to cover up or revise the historical truth, a number of variations (e.g., "Hard Rock", "Rock", "Punk Rock", "Heavy Metal", etc.) of the term and style of Rock and Roll (aka "nigger" music) has been created and promoted as "original" forms of American music created by white Americans and unrelated to "nigger" music.

This ongoing fraud is a profoundly unethical and amoral act that infects the American character. It represents one of a list of such misconduct that has caused the world – especially the world's non-white population – to lose respect for and trust in America. It is such misconduct that has created the image of the "ugly American". Furthermore, such morally shameful behavior unfairly makes all white Americans look like people who cannot be trusted, who are morally incapable of putting the truth ahead of their own selfish advantage. And although such a generalization is unfair, it undoubtedly contributes to the anti-American propaganda of America as an ungodly and selfishly destructive culture.

In any case, there seems to be but one effective antibiotic against this insidiously chronic moral infection of American social ethics. That antibiotic is the truth. And it must be applied persistently until it is the prevailing story in the historical record, including that of Rock and Roll, aka Rhythm and Blues, aka "nigger" music.